MAR   2018

Polish Chicken

by Joyce Markovics

Consultant: Darin Collins, DVM
Director, Animal Health Programs
Woodland Park Zoo
Seattle, Washington

BEARPORT
PUBLISHING

New York, New York

Credits

Cover, © Eric Isselee/Shutterstock, © NEstudio/Shutterstock, and © Voronin76/Shutterstock; TOC, © Eric Isselee/Shutterstock; 4–5, © Jean-Michel Labat/Arden; 6L, © Eric Isselee/Shutterstock; 6–7, © Keith J Smith/Alamy Stock Photo; 8L, © Olhastock/Shutterstock; 8R, © Stefan Petru Andronache/Shutterstock; 9, © alan1951/Fotolia and © pimchawee/Shutterstock; 9B, Public Domain; 10T, © Msibley/Dreamstime; 10B, © Cynoclub/Dreamstime; 11 (L to R), © Justine Pickett/Alamy Stock Photo, © Hoovie918/iStock, and © dennisvdw/iStock; 12, © Eric Isselee/Shutterstock; 12–13, © Nik Taylor Wildlife/Alamy Stock Photo; 14, © Isselee/Dreamstime; 15, © Stefan Andronache/Dreamstime; 16, © Tierfotoagentur/Alamy Stock Photo; 17 (T to B), © mlorenz/Shutterstock, © Jim Cumming/Shutterstock, and © Eric Isselee/Shutterstock; 18, © Nicole Spencer/Dreamstime; 19, © Sundrycreations/Dreamstime; 20L, © Eric Isselee/Shutterstock; 20–21, © Nicole Spencer/Dreamstime; 22 (T to B), © Einar Muoni/Shutterstock, © Diandra Dills/CC BY-SA 3.0, and © cynoclub/Shutterstock; 23TL, © Menna/Shutterstock; 23TR, © David Havel/Shutterstock; 23BL, Public Domain; 23BR, © MISHELLA/Shutterstock; Back Cover, © Eric Isselee/Shutterstock.

Publisher: Kenn Goin
Senior Editor: Joyce Tavolacci
Creative Director: Spencer Brinker
Design: Debrah Kaiser
Photo Researcher: Thomas Persano

Library of Congress Cataloging-in-Publication Data

Names: Markovics, Joyce L., author.
Title: Polish chicken / by Joyce Markovics.
Description: New York, New York : Bearport Publishing, [2018] | Series: Weirder and cuter | Audience: Ages 5–8. | Includes bibliographical references and index.
Identifiers: LCCN 2017012105 (print) | LCCN 2017005088 (ebook) | ISBN 9781684022625 (library) | ISBN 9781684023165 (Ebook)
Subjects: LCSH: Chickens—Juvenile literature. | Chicken breeds—Juvenile literature.
Classification: LCC SF487.5 .M3727 2018 (ebook) | LCC SF487.5 (print) | DDC 636.5—dc23
LC record available at https://lccn.loc.gov/2017012105

For more information, write to Bearport Publishing Company, Inc., 45 West 21st Street, Suite 3B, New York, New York 10010. Printed in the United States of America.

10 9 8 7 6 5 4 3 2 1

Contents

What's this weird but cute animal?

It's a **Polish chicken.**

4

Big,
fluffy
crest!

Scaly feet!

5

How big is a Polish chicken?

The bird is about the size of a Chihuahua.

A Polish chicken can weigh up to 5 pounds (2.3 kg).

Polish chickens don't look like other chickens.

Why?

They have big **tufts** of feathers on their heads.

common chicken

Polish chicken

This bunch of feathers is called a crest.

knob on skull

A Polish chicken has a knob, or bump, on its **skull**. The crest grows from skin that covers the knob.

9

There are many varieties of Polish chickens.

Some have curly feathers.

Others have long feathers on their necks.

Polish chickens come in many colors.

Chickens scratch the ground with their feet.

They're looking for tasty bugs to eat!

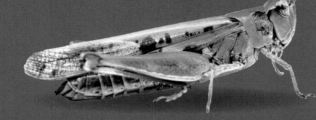

They also gobble up seeds and vegetables.

Chickens do not have teeth. They swallow tiny stones, which help them grind up their food.

Male Polish chickens, or roosters, like to dance when they eat!

They make sounds and move their heads up and down.

This dance is called tidbitting.

Peep!
Chirp!

Squawk!
Hiss!

Chickens can make about 30 **distinct** sounds.

If the birds see a **predator** on the ground, they let out a warning cry.

That cry changes
if the enemy is
in the sky!

Owls, foxes,
and skunks all
hunt chickens.

Some Polish chickens can't see their enemies very well.

Their crests are so large they cover the birds' eyes!

To help a bird see, its owner can carefully trim its crest.

These wacky chickens make great pets.

They're gentle and friendly.

They enjoy cuddling with their human friends!

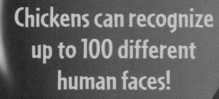

Chickens can recognize up to 100 different human faces!

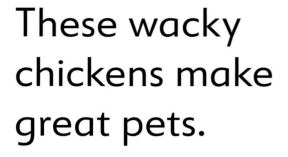

More Weird Chickens

ear tufts

Araucana Chicken
Araucana chickens from Chile lay blue eggs. Sometimes, they have big tufts of feathers growing out of their ears!

Onagadori Chicken
Onagadori chickens come from Japan. They have super long tail feathers that can grow up to 12 feet (3.7 m)!

Silkie Chicken
These fluffy chickens are covered with silky feathers that look like fur. Silkies are known for their black skin, flesh, and bones!

Glossary

distinct (dih-STINGKT) different

predator (PRED-uh-tur) an animal that hunts and eats other animals

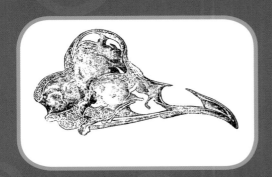

skull (SKUHL) the part of the skeleton that forms the head

tufts (TUHFTS) bunches or clumps of feathers

Index

Read More

Lundgren, Julie. *Chickens (Life Cycles).* Vero Beach, FL: Rourke (2011).

Markovics, Joyce. *Chicken (See Them Grow).* New York: Bearport (2017).

Learn More Online

To learn more about Polish chickens, visit
www.bearportpublishing.com/WeirderandCuter

About the Author

Joyce Markovics lives along the Hudson River in a very old house. She often wonders whether a Polish chicken and her feisty pet rabbit, Pearl, would get along.